SPOT

AROUND TOWN

BUS STATION

by Alissa Thielges

amicus LEARNING

kiosk

ramp

Look for these words and pictures as you read.

shelter

map

Let's go to the bus station.
What will we see?

kiosk

Look at the kiosk.
Nina buys a pass.
Now she can ride the bus.

U
BUS
Tram
S
Tickets
MVV
MVG
Tickets
Bitte Bildschirm berühren!
Please touch the screen!
Abbruch
easy
ICA

RR4-Hyde Park
8088S
MONDEGO H
GAUTRAIN
BC 34 SH GP

Buses drive around town.
You can get on at a bus stop.

CITY BUS ROUTES
ROUTE 1
ROUTE 2
ROUTE 3
ROUTE 4
ROUTE 5
ROUTE 6

map

Look at the map.
It shows the bus routes.
Where will you go?

ramp

Look at the ramp.
A woman rides in a wheelchair.
It is easy to get on.

64-501

Look at the shelter.
It covers the benches.
Max stays dry.

shelter

A bus leaves the station.
It will stop at the library next.
See you there!

kiosk

ramp

Did you find?

map

shelter

SPOT

Spot is published by Amicus Learning, an imprint of Amicus
P.O. Box 227, Mankato, MN 56002
www.amicuspublishing.us

Library of Congress Cataloging-in-Publication Data
Names: Thielges, Alissa, 1995- author.
Title: Bus station / by Alissa Thielges.
Description: Mankato : Amicus Learning, [2024] | Series: Spot around town | Audience: Ages 4–7 | Audience: Grades K–1 | Summary: "A search-and-find book about bus stations reinforces new vocabulary to build reading success while close-up images of places and buildings captivate young audiences. A great book to inspire learning about communities on field trips for kindergartners and first graders"—Provided by publisher.
Identifiers: LCCN 2023039316 (print) | LCCN 2023039317 (ebook) | ISBN 9781645497325 (library binding) | ISBN 9781645497400 (ebook)
Subjects: LCSH: Bus terminals—Juvenile literature. | Buses—Juvenile literature.
Classification: LCC HE5611 .T45 2024 (print) | LCC HE5611 (ebook) | DDC 388.3/4233—dc23/eng/0824
LC record available at https://lccn.loc.gov/2023039316
LC ebook record available at https://lccn.loc.gov/2023039317

Printed in China

Rebecca Glaser, editor
Deb Miner, series designer
Kim Pfeffer, book designer and photo researcher

Photos by Alamy/Clearpix, 12–13, Florian Peljak/Süddeutsche Zeitung Photo, 5; Depositphotos/RichTphoto, 6–7; Dreamstime, Mauro Rodrigues, 1; iStock/hjurcik, 3, JordiRamisa, 10–11, vm, 8–9; Shutterstock/Fotokon, cover, Jeka, 5; Wikimedia Commons/Beantowndude316, 14

BUS STATION